INTERIOR. ANSIEDAD. NOCHE.

Lucy Caraballo

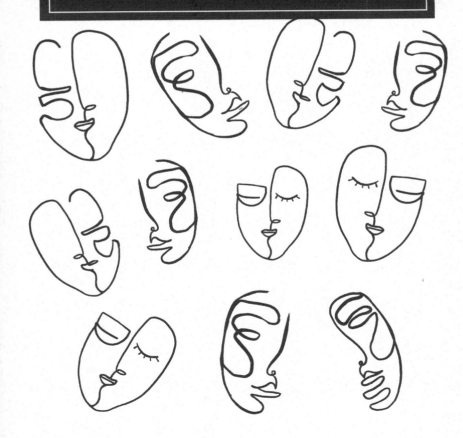

Créditos / Credits

Interior. Anxiety. Night.
(c) Texto / Text 2020,
Lucy Caraballo

(c) Ilustraciones / Illustrations 2021,
Amy Cabrero

Dirección de diseño y diagramación /
Design direction & diagramming,
Jeniffer Pace, CAVE Design Studio

Editora / Editor,
Alejandra Ramos

Para información / For information:
by.lucycaraballo@gmail.com
ISBN: 978-1-09837-750-2

Este libro es sobre mi experiencia personal y pensamientos sobre la ansiedad. No soy un profesional de la salud mental y no tengo un título en salud mental.

El contenido de este libro contiene poemas y pensamientos sobre enfermedades mentales y crisis de salud mental, específicos sobre el trastorno de ansiedad social y el trastorno de ansiedad generalizada, que algunos lectores pueden encontrar desencadenantes.

Si necesita ayuda en cualquier momento, llame a la Red Nacional de Prevención del Suicidio Lifeline al 1-888-628-9454 (en español) o al 1-800-273-8255 (en inglés), o envíe un mensaje en inglés a la línea de crisis para mensajes de texto (con la palabra HELLO al 741741). Ambos servicios son gratuitos y están disponibles 24 horas al día, 7 días a la semana. Las personas sordas o con problemas de audición pueden comunicarse con Lifeline por TTY al 1-800-799-4889. Todas las llamadas son confidenciales.

****

This book is about my own personal experience and thoughts on anxiety. I'm not an mental health professional and I do not have a degree in mental health.

Content in this book contains poems and thoughts of mental illness and mental health crisis, specific about SAD (social anxiety disorder) and GAD (Generalized Anxiety Disorder), which some readers may find triggering.

If you need support at any time, please call the National Suicide Prevention Hotline at 1-800-273-TALK or text the Crisis Text Line (text HELLO to 741741). Both services are free and available 24 hours a day, seven days a week. The deaf and hard of hearing can contact the Lifeline via TTY at 1-800-799-4889. All calls are confidential.

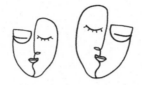

This book is dedicated to my father,
Miguel A. Caraballo,
for teaching me about unconditional love,
his support, his strength through his
fight with Cancer, and his courage.
He passed away in 2016, but he still lives
in my heart.

También le dedico este libro a mi Madre,
Luz E. Caraballo,
por enseñarme lo que es el amor
incondicional,
su fuerza al estar ahí con mi Papá hasta
lo último, y su apoyo.

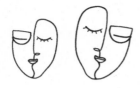

This book was written as an automatic page turner that I couldn't put down. Lucy does an exquisite job, not only as a writer, but as an artist who painted everlasting images that become part of your memory.

Color psychology is used as personification in "Playing with Demons" to differentiate the emotions that exist for her during mental episodes. "Speak" exposes feelings that I know all too well from when your mind wants to take action, but your lips won't move. When reading "Peace", I asked myself if my demons and my angels co-existed in every moment of life with me, or if spirits also have to take breaks. This makes you question, what part of your body is actually in control during these experiences. How well do you know yourself? And, how will you behave in every situation?

In reading this piece of work, you will be able to recall moments in time where you have seen people live through mental episodes, but weren't able to describe what was in front of you in words, until now.

Quameisha Moreno
Author and Writing Teacher

Bienvenidos a pensamientos y palabras que habitan dentro de una mente con ansiedad.

Ya que mi mundo y mis pensamientos usualmente son en inglés y en español, he decidido escribir un libro bilingüe, y compartir mis pensamientos en ambos idiomas.

Escribo este libro para que aquellos que no sufren de ansiedad entiendan cómo funciona nuestra mente. Y con la esperanza de ayudar a que las personas que tienen ansiedad se sientan identificadas y sepan que no están solos. Yo no lo estoy, tú tampoco.

* * * * * * * *

Welcome to the thoughts and words inside an anxious mind.

Given that my world and my thoughts usually happen in English and Spanish, I decided to write a bilingual book and share my thoughts in both languages. This book hopes to shed light to those who don't have anxiety to understand or at least peak inside an anxious mind, and wishes for people with anxiety to feel "seen" and understood. I hope that by reading this book you can see you are not alone. I am not and neither are you.

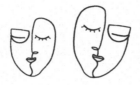

PENSAMIENTOS DE LA MEDIANOCHE

Escribo para saber cómo bregar con todo
esto. Me estoy ahogando. No en una playa,
piscina, o bañera. Ni en un lago, un río,
ni ningún cuerpo grande o pequeño de agua,
sino en un vaso. Sí, en un vaso. "Vaso medio
lleno" diría un optimista, "un vaso medio
vacío" diría un pesimista, "un vaso con agua
a mitad" diría un realista. Pero Ansiedad
dice "te estás ahogando, siente eso, estás
sin aire, apenas respiras. Sí, te ahogas".
Y te das cuenta de que te ahogas llena
de miedos y mentiras. Maldita ansiedad.
Maldita.

I am writing to see how to take all these
feelings out of me. I am drowning. Not in a
beach, not in a pool, not in a bathtub. It's
not a lake, neither is a river, it is not
any big or small body of water, instead, a
glass. Yes, a glass. "Glass half full" would
say an optimist. "Glass half empty" would
say a pessimist."A glass with water halfway"
would say the realist. But Anxiety says
"You are drowning, feel it, you are without
air, you can't barely breathe. Yes, you are
drowning." And you notice just then you
are drowning in your fears and lies. Damn,
anxiety. Damn.

Debería dormir. Descansar. Dejar que la
mente deje de pensar. Pero no, a esta hora
es que ella quiere resolver todos los
problemas o, mejor dicho, crear problemas,
hacerlos gigantes y hacerte sentir que
estás atrapada en las cuatro paredes de tu
casa, de tu cuarto, sin salida, sin aire.
Ella vuelve todo negativo, negro, oscuro.
Te grita y te da dolor de cabeza. "¿Dormir?
¡JA! No me hagas reír", dice Ansiedad.
"Quizás cuando no piense más, ella dormirá",
me digo. Y, Ansiedad responde, "nos vemos
mañana, a la misma hora y en el mismo
lugar".

I should sleep. Let my mind rest and stop
thinking. But no, this is when she decides
to solve all the problems, or even worse,
to create problems, make them bigger,
scarier, and make you feel trapped in the
four walls of your house, of your room, with
no exit, no air. The mind sees everything
as negative, black, obscure. She yells,
giving you a headache, and says, "Sleep? HA!
Don't make me laugh". And I say to myself,
"this will only happen after you exhaust
your mind, only then sleep will come". But
Anxiety responds, "Don't worry there is
always tomorrow, same time and same place".

El silencio molesta. Me inquieta. Da libre albedrío a mis demonios. De noche escucho más duro sus voces, durante el día controlo mejor el volumen. De día tengo el control, de noche lo pierdo. Por la noche, quieta, buscando ese sueño que no llega, peleando para dormirme, ellas, las voces, esas voces, ven la oportunidad de tomar el centro, coger el control y gritar. Escupen todo lo negativo, me llenan de oscuridad. A veces duermo con la luz encendida, tratando de espantarlas, de que huyan. Mientras trato de buscar el sueño, cuento ovejas, respiro, y me digo, "duerme, que así se alejan las voces, pronto la mañana regresará y podrás tomar el control. Calma, solo duerme, que ellas callarán. Mañana será otro día".

The silence bothers me, makes me feel restless. It gives free will to my demons. At night I hear their voices stronger than during the day. During the day I can control their volume. At nighttime, I lose it. At night. Still. Silent. Trying to fall asleep while struggling with them, the voices. They see the opportunity to take center stage, take control, and they scream, they yell out negative thoughts, feeling me up with darkness. Sometimes I sleep with the light on, trying to scare them away, make them run. While I'm trying to sleep, to breathe, I say to myself: "they will go away, soon morning will come, you'll have the control again, calm, just sleep, they will shut up. Tomorrow it's a new day."

Pienso. ¿Por qué realmente creo que compartir mis palabras, mis pensamientos, es interesante o importante? Complejidad. Oscuridad. Miedos. Intensidad. Realismo. Dolor. Ansiedad. ¿A quién realmente le interesaría leer esto? ¿Alguien puede identificarse conmigo? ¿Con mis pensamientos, mis miedos, mis demonios? ¿Sí? ¿Cómo, si son míos? Nada especial. Nada importante. Solo son palabras y nada más. ¿Valdrá la pena? ¿Tendrá sentido? ¿Objetivo?

I think and think. Is it really important for me to choose to share my words, my thoughts? Are they interesting or relevant? Complexity. Darkness. Fears. Intensity. Realism. Pain. Anxiety. Who would really be interested in reading this? Could anyone identify with me? With my words, my thoughts, my fears, my demons? Yes? But why? They are just my thoughts, nothing special. Nothing important. They are just words and nothing more. Is it worth it? Would it make sense? Would it have a purpose? An objective?

Este encierro, esta preocupación, incertidumbre, este miedo real versus el miedo que añade la ansiedad. No más, no puedo más, duerme ya. Ya no sé qué es real y qué no. Ya no sé cuándo es miedo y cuándo es ansiedad. ¿Qué es real? No le tengo miedo a morir, pero sí miedo a los que sufrirían mi muerte. El dolor, mi sufrimiento, mi desespero, eso no se lo deseo a nadie. Ya no puedo más. No más, por favor, duerme ya. He tenido noches donde he pensado cómo sería quedarme dormida. Si despertara en otra vida, ¿cómo sería?. Esta oscuridad, este mar de pensamientos, esta soledad, esta ansiedad que me ahoga... no me deja respirar. No más. Ya, por favor, duerme ya. Duerme.

1:24 am: No more, sleep now!

This confinement, this concern, this worry, this uncertainty, this fear plus the fear added by the anxiety. No more. I can't. I need to sleep. I don't know what is real and what is not, anymore. I don't know if it's fear or anxiety. What is real? I am not scared to die, but I do fear the pain my loved ones will have because of my death. This pain, the hurt, the despair... I don't wish it to anyone. I honestly can't hold this anymore. I can't. No more. Please, I need to sleep. I've had nights where I've thought how it would be if I stayed asleep... if I woke up in the next life, how would it be? This darkness, this sea of thoughts, this loneliness, it drowns me to a point I can't breathe. No more, please. Sleep now. Sleep.

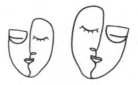

Poemas en español / Spanish Poems

Ahora, por favor disfruten de mis poemas
en español.

* * * * * * * *

Now, please enjoy my poems in Spanish.

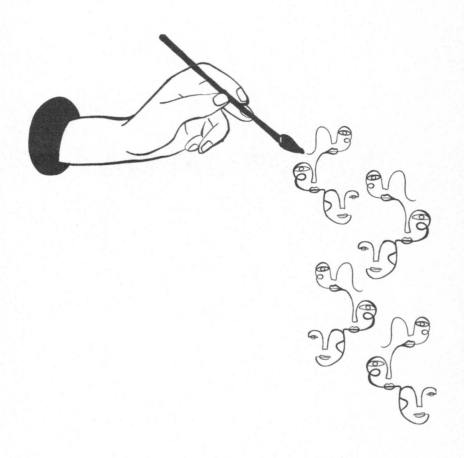

Palabras

No encuentro las palabras
Quiero escribir y no sale nada
Intento expresar
Pero no encuentro las palabras

Me ahogo en el silencio
Grito al vacío, al viento
Nadie me escucha

Ansiedad
Miedos
Voces que mienten
Miedo que engaña
Odio
Total vacío
Sin palabras

Proceso
Entendimientos
Contexto
Pensamientos

He intentado abrirme
He intentado hablar
Quizás ya olvidé cómo
Porque hablo solo con soledad

Corro para no encontrar
Que al final no tengo a nadie
Que jamás dejé que vieran
Mi dolor, mi soledad

¿Y si ya soy solo un fantasma?
¿Y si ya no existo?
¿Y si por eso es que no me escuchan?
¿Y ya no vivo?

Voces

Me pregunto de dónde vienen
Todos estos pensamientos
Tanto dolor, tanto miedo
Tantas voces

Lucho contra mis voces
Que me dicen que no soy suficiente
Que jamás lo seré
Que no vale la pena luchar por cambiar
Pensamientos negativos que nunca se irán
Voces

No sentir amor
Solo dolor
No sentir vida
Solo sufrimiento, vacío

Y siento que me rindo
Que no encuentro la salida
Qué más da luchar
Si todo esto siempre será igual
Voces continuarán

Sin Sentido

Soy débil
Mis demonios ganan
Sin sentido de vivir
Sin las ganas

Aglomerada por los pensamientos
Pienso en todo lo que he fallado
Pienso en todo lo que no he logrado
Pensamiento tras pensamiento

Siento que no pertenezco
En este mundo sin lugar
Vida sin interés
Sin sentido

Grito en silencio
Sin aire
Sin sonido
Todo sigue
Sin sentido

Tiempo

El tiempo pasa
Entiendo que las cosas
Se olvidan
La rutina gana
Ten cuidado
Ella también mata

Un mar de sentimientos
Un par de pensamientos
Mientras el tiempo pasa
Menos sé qué traerá el mañana

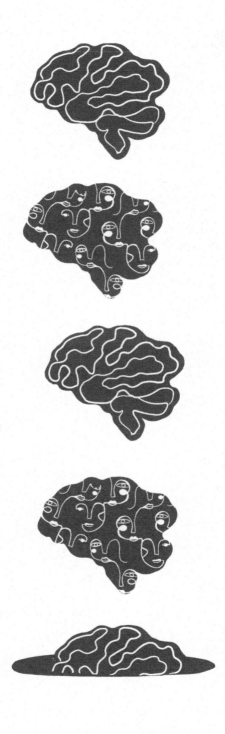

Miedo

Un miedo incontrolable
Es indescriptible, no hay palabras
Un miedo que no cambia
Que paraliza el alma

Demonios o ángeles
Oscuro, vacío, sin fondo
Voces que gritan y no callan
Maldita ansiedad
Ansiedad que mata
Ansiedad que no calla

Cayendo

¿Alguna vez has odiado tu vida, tu cuerpo,
tu mente, tu corazón, tu todo?
¿Alguna vez pensaste que no puedes más?

Pensar tan negativo que no quieres pensar más
Caer sin encontrar final
¿Cuándo tocarás el fondo?

Sigues cayendo y cayendo
Gritas, pero no sale voz
Tienes miedo, quieres llorar
Sigues cayendo
Todo en tu pecho
Sin poder hablar ni gritar

Y sigues cayendo
Y no hay final
Y sigues cayendo
Quiero parar
No sentir más
Y aún sigues cayendo...

Espejo

Evito el espejo
El reflejo
Que refleja todo lo que pienso

No quiero ver
Los demonios
¿Dónde se fueron los ángeles?
No los veo

Tantos oscuros pensamientos
Tantos miedos
¿Cómo puedo ser quien soy?
Cuando ni siquiera conozco
La mujer del espejo

Identidad
Destino
Vida
Realidad

Al final, ¿cómo me encuentro?
¿Cómo sé quién soy?
¿A quién veo en el reflejo?
¿Quién es la mujer en el espejo?

Mano a mano

De mano a mano voy
De una mano con ansiedad
De otra con depresión
Caminando sin parar

Miento cuando digo que estoy bien
Miento, lo admito
Nadie puede entender
El sufrimiento, el dolor

¿Cómo apagar la mente?
¿Cómo callar las voces?
¿Cómo decirles que necesitas silencio?

Buscas una salida
Y la salida no aparece
A veces pienso cerrar los ojos
Dormir
No despertar
A ver si así se callan las voces

Mi piel

Huyo de mis demonios
Por miedo a mirar
Escondo todo
Por miedo a mirar
No quiero aceptar
Lo que no puedo cambiar

Mi piel quema
Me incomoda
Si pudiera quitarla
Si pudiera cambiarla

No puedo amar
Lo que no amo
No puedo ser entera
Porque solo soy mitad
La otra no existe

Huyo de mis demonios
Corro sin mirar atrás
Escondida de todo
Sin ganas de parar

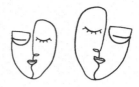

From Español to English:

Ahora los invito a mi mundo en inglés.
Escribí todos los poemas anteriores en
español para recuperar mi lengua materna
pero tengo que aceptar que fue un gran reto.
El inglés se me hace ya más natural que el
español. Esto quizás se vea mal porque yo
crecí en Puerto Rico. Pero ahora vivo en
Nueva York y el inglés es la lengua que más
uso aunque todavía me comunico en español
con mi familia en la isla. La realidad es
que ambos idiomas son parte de mí, ambos me
representan, en ambos me comunico y aunque
son distintos, expresan la misma ansiedad.
Así que a partir de ahora leerán mis poemas
escritos originalmente en inglés.

* * * * * * * *

Now I welcome you to my world in English.
Until now you've read my thoughts and poems
about anxiety in Spanish which was a big
challenge since, as bad as it might sound,
it is easier for me to write in English
although I grew up in Puerto Rico. I still
speak Spanish with my family in New York and
it is my mother language so it was important
to express myself and my anxiety in both
languages. The reality is I live in both
worlds and both make sense to me, both speak
to me, both represent me and offer me unique
ways of expression, and different ways to
open myself up. From now on you will read my
poems written originally in English.

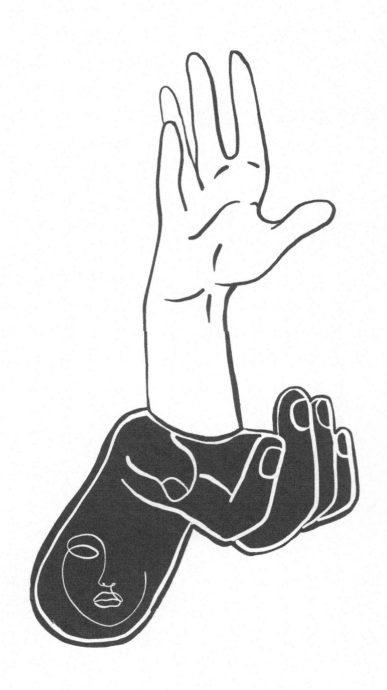

Not Enough

Some have an angel and a devil
Talking in their shoulders
Anxiety makes me feel
My angel was replaced
Leaving me with two devils instead

Noises, can't turn off
Feelings, can't stop
Pain, I can't control
Hate, all that I've known

My skin is not mine
I would use a knife to take it off
I can't stand this feeling
It's overwhelming
My skin is burning
But I am not a snake
My skin isn't changing

Not enough
Daughter, sister
Friend, neighbor
Cousin, student
Artist
Any?
All?
The feeling lives
I am not enough

Am I worth of
Compassion, a companion
Friendship, family, love?

Am I enough?

Voices in my head

I can't quiet the voices in my head
They shout all night
Can't sleep, can't cry
The emotions hide inside

I want to run
I want to hide
I want to live
I want to die

It's killing me slowly
It's taking my soul
An invisible demon
Silencing my voice

My skin is not mine
I lost myself
I scream
But no sound comes out

I need to ask for help
I need to save myself
In order for this to end

Not now

I shout out loud inside
Quiet!
I am in control
Quiet!

Not now
I said
Fears
Years
I'm scared

I came out of the hole
Out of the darkness
Not more hiding
Not now I said

Fears
They won't control me
Breathe
Stay still

You are strong
Put the armor
Take the sword
Be ready to fight
Fears, not now I said

Stronger
Wiser
The pain
The hurt
Lessons learned

Fears
Anxiety
Not now
Not now I said

Uncertainty

I lost myself
Standing in a road
With no direction

Where to turn?
Right for dreams
Left for security
Back for comfort
Front for uncertainty

Life is full of surprises
I never expect anything
I know pain and I know emptiness
But where is happiness?

Uncertainty
Loneliness
Silence
Lost
Pain

Waiting for a sign
Standing still
Uncertain is the future
Unanswered questions
Waiting still

Roller coaster

Down to the black hole
Up to optimism
Backwards to fears
The upfront scares me

Up and down
Dark and light
Voices, quiet!
Your screaming is so loud!

They stop
Only for a moment
False security
I am about to take the seat belt off
And the ride will start again

Up and down
Loud screams
Quiet, I said
Let me think
I need to catch a breath

Stop
Let me out
I can't take another ride
On life
On this roller coaster of life

Darkness

I am in a dark hole
Of emptiness
Sadness
And darkness

I need guidance
Someone who can help me
Help me see the light
Help me see a way out
Because I can't see none

I don't see a point
To keep living like this
The thoughts, the feelings
I'm tired of it all

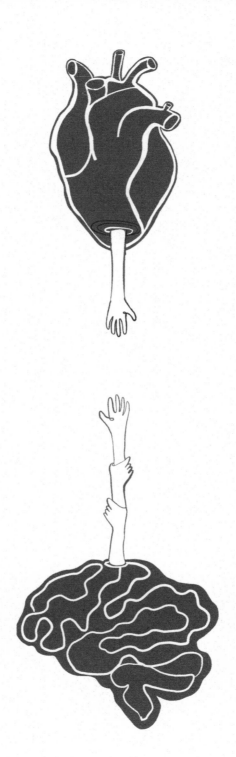

Brain circuit

Wires connected
Circuits defected
Brain unprotected
Electricity undetected

There is a new way
Maybe a new perspective
To develop, to control
The thoughts, the fears
To perceive threats undetected

I get triggered
When the fears appear
But it's a chemical imbalance
A brain response
To a fake threat
I can't control
This is the new way
I manage to work
Brain circuits
In them, all

Overwhelmed

Overwhelmed with darkness
Powerless
Stillness
Noises arise

Overwhelmed with sadness
Heartache
Pain
Broken

Overwhelmed with silence

Deaf to the world
Inside, voices scream
So loud they can break a glass
But remain unheard by the outside world

Overwhelmed
Overwhelmed
Overwhelmed
What is there to be done?

I don't care

They seemed worried
They asked and wondered
The outsiders
The strangers

I reached out
I jumped
I danced
I screamed
No one listened

They said they care
They asked me to listen
But I saw them through my heart
They had the "I don't care" look

And I kept on dancing
With my demons

Personalities

Have you ever met me when I'm anxious?
Or do you only see me in my best days?

There are different faces
Some are scary as hell
Others are sweet and innocent
I'm scared
I'm in pain

The optimist believes it is helpful
To think

The scared one thinks it is hurtful
To speak

The innocent thinks it is not harmful
To express

The scary one is hurtful
It makes me write words
Words I'm not brave enough to say

They all live inside me
None of them in charge
Maybe the scary one thinks she is
But the voices speak
All at the same time
Making everyone weak

The personalities
The faces
The fears
That live in my mind
Everyday

Pain

I dance with my pain
I know her secrets
And she knows mine

We fight
We scream at each other
We don't hold back
The words hurt so badly

I keep repeating
"I can handle my pain,
I am okay,
And I can handle it somehow"

Pain comes in waves
There is one that hurts the most
Grief
The loss of someone
Someone you'll never get back

Tears don't come out
But I feel my heart breaking
A little more every day
Every night
Pain lives in me
And I handle it somehow

Playing with demons

I gave them names
They have personalities
Now I'm never alone
Now there's all but silence

Blue is the saddest
She sees everything grey
She is hopeless, unlovable

Yellow wants hope
She lives in a borderline
Scared to cross it
But hopeful to do so

Black is darkness
She scares them all
She enjoys the pain
She hurts them

White is innocent
White is the pure that it's left
She tries to bring lightness
To Black, Blue, and Yellow

Purple is my favorite
She is optimistic
She learned to live with the others
She keeps them in check
She is not scared of the darkness

All my demons
Lives inside me
Sometimes they burn
Sometimes I feel dead
They all own me
But I am not scared of them
I now know them
My demons have names

Hold my hand

I hold hands with my demons
One hand for depression
One hand for anxiety
Hand in hand we walk

They don't understand
I explain but they don't listen
Maybe I don't explain it right

I can't sleep
I'm awake at 2am
Thoughts running through my mind
I can't shut them out

I want to shut them off
I want the voices to stop
They don't seem to know
They don't see how hard I try

I walk holding hands with my demons
I try to be tough
I want to show control
Be brave, it will be alright

Loneliness

A roommate no one wants
She is heavy, takes space
Speaks her mind, my truth

She dwells all day
Eats carbs, stays in bed
Drinks, eats
Takes all that's mine

She is selfish
She hates company
She hates outside noises
And calls no one

I grew accustomed to her
I am comfortable now
I am okay with her
Sharing my space
Even though it doesn't feel right

Loneliness
Emptiness
Is it good?
Is it bad?

It's hard when neither she nor I have the
answers
What now? What can be said or done?
Who has the answers?
Should I tell her to leave and never come
back?
It's a company I crave but never seek
Anyways, I stay with her
Loneliness and I

Peace

I found peace
When I accepted darkness
They both danced happily inside

I dreamed of peace
Garden, clouds,
A beautiful place
It turns out to be a forest
Day time is beautiful
Nighttime falls into darkness

Amid all
I found peace
Accepting the dark
The voices were silenced

Grateful
Peace is welcomed
I long for it
Still getting used to it
Peace

Complex

Complex feelings
Complex thoughts
Uncontrolled feelings
My mind doesn't stop

Have you ever fallen to a point you are
unable to stand?
Have you ever eaten finding yourself unable
to swallow?

The grey cloud
Follows me around
I don't carry an umbrella anymore
I love the rain hitting my skin
I love to feel the pain when it touches me

Complex
To be vocal
Complex
To feel

It's hard
To understand
The complexity
To understand
The fears
A necessary step to be free
A most likely step into uncertainty

Speak

"Speak", said the therapist
"Let it out"
"Feel it"
"Speak"

But I can't find the words
My thoughts are running at 100 miles per
hour
In a highway full of fears

The puzzle has a thousand pieces
The colors all look alike
How can I pick one?
What if it's the wrong one?

I miss the quiet times
I miss not knowing what I now know I have:
anxiety

"Speak", said the therapist
But I have no words
"Speak"
But I can't
"Speak"
I'm frozen
"Speak"
Why? She doesn't listen
"Speak"
Ok. I'll try one more time

My own thoughts

Terrified
I shut my eyes
I can't look
I wish they'd all go away

Fears
Anxiety
Pain
Hurt

Lost in my own thoughts
There is no control
No button to shut off
No place to hide

How can I escape?
Trapped in my body
Trapped in my mind
No place to hide

My own thoughts
My own enemies
There is no love
Only fear

My brain, my mind
Are they not working right?
There is a wire broken
Can't trust them
My own thoughts
My fears
Escape, I say

Mirror

I stand up in front of the mirror
I am standing up for myself
Hello voices
Hello demons

You make me feel worthless
You speak fears and hurt
Don't you see you are hurting?
Be gentle with myself

Stop and listen
It's me who needs to speak

You like to put me in the darkness
I am stopping you
I won't let you hurt me

Mirrors reflect voices
Mirrors reflect noises
Mirrors reflect nothingness
I see the emptiness

I stand and I am broken
I put my force shield
I hit the mirror, the fist starts to bleed
Relief,
The feeling of broken
It's now reflected in the broken mirror
instead
I am no longer in my head
Real touch
Blood
The pain is real
I am showing you the way I feel
The broken mirror reflects it

Afraid

Afraid of who I've become
Afraid of who I am
Hide, don't show
Darkness inside

Half a person
How can I be who I am?
I'm burning inside
I think the other half is gone

I'm afraid to love because I've never known
it
How am I supposed to love?
If I've never had someone show me love before

Afraid to love
Afraid to lose
Afraid to say
Afraid to feel
Afraid to look ahead
Afraid to look back

How can I be who I am?
When fears come
Overwhelming me
I'm afraid to be who I am

Still

Stand still
Listen to the wind
Quiet the voices
Listen, don't speak

Stillness
Emptiness
Don't move
Don't speak

The devil is inside
Playing cards
Speaking voices
Please don't listen

Avoid
Don't make contact
Don't look back
There is nothing
There are only memories

Be still
Breathe
This moment
It will pass
Listen, breathe
Don't speak

Balance

There is a scale
An invisible line
Sweet, delicate balance

There is goodness inside
There is bad as well
Decisions, decisions
Invisible line
Impossible balance

Delicate balance
If I could take medicine
If I could be the balance myself
Make life easier, make it simple
Balance, delicate balance
Needed to create

The other side

Words can heal
Can hurt
Can burn
Can scare

The power of words
The power on you
You must heal yourself

Happiness is possible
Optimism is key
Light a candle
To see the other side of darkness
Find the light within you

My own savior

For years I've been my own worst enemy
I've been waiting for a savior

Years waiting for a miracle
A friend, a family
A stranger, a lover
A doctor, a teacher
Only to find out
I had to be
My own savior

Only I can save myself
If I get to the top to jump
If I get close to the dark
Only I can find the light

Years blinded
Thinking
I couldn't be
My own savior
I was my own hater
Love was not near

Years to understand
Only I can save myself
Love is here
I just need to shut down the voices
And stand up to fear

I am my own savior
Not just today
Every day
Every night
Fighting battles no one sees
No one knows
I will win some
I will lose others
What matters is
To never give up
I am my own savior

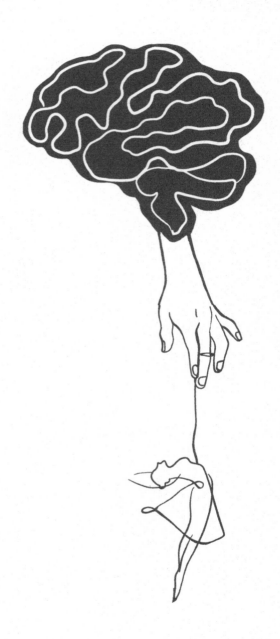

Same old me

Some old
Others new
Some, somewhere in between

Same old me
Same old fears
Same routine
Old and new

When I thought I knew me
There is a new me that comes out
New thoughts appear
But I'm always back to the same old me

I try to explain my fears
I try to understand my pain
How can you explain something you barely
understand?
How to understand pain?
I'm filled with feelings I can't explain
How do I express myself?

Unseen, unheard, unspoken

You know the image of the monkey?
Hands on eyes, mouth, and ears?
Can't see, can't speak, can't hear
Unseen, unheard, unspoken

Unseen, the wish
To change the things I've seen
The things that hurt
The things that scare me

Unheard, the want
To change the things I've heard
The things that cause me pain
The ones that broke me

Unspoken, the need
To change the things I've said
Things that cause others pain
Things I should have never said

Deep inside
I wish I had seen the love
I wish I had heard the voices
I wish I spoke the truth
Don't we all wish to have a chance?
A chance to be seen, to be heard?
A chance to speak?

Versions of myself

Like a phoenix
Part of yourself will die
Part will be back
You will survive

There are so many versions of myself
Some versions never see the light
Some versions hide, scared
Some versions run and never come back

I bear the pain
It is not long enough
Until I learn to let go
And discover It's okay to do so
I sit and listen
Each version has its own pain
Its own fear
Its own scar
Sit and listen, it's okay to let go

Leave it behind
Overcome it
Feel stronger
A new version
An old one to leave behind
Always multiple lives living inside
your mind
Multiple versions of myself

Clear mind

Inner peace
Silencing the voices
Listening to my gut
Trusting myself

Clearing my mind
Imagining a beautiful empty space
Oceans, gardens
Perhaps me being above clouds
Clearing my mind

Trusting to know what's right
Not letting my fears
Or voices
Tell me otherwise

Clearing my mind
Listening to my heart
Telling me I have the power
To take it back
Silencing the voices
Clearing my mind

Tomorrow

Night comes
Full of darkness
And it brings the thoughts
Full of fears and hate

The grey cloud turns black
The room feels smaller
The world seems bigger
I feel worthless

I turn off the lights
Letting the night come my way
Listening to sad songs
Escaping the world
Getting lost in darkness
Letting it consume me

The night understands me
The dark welcomes me
Tomorrow they will come
And so will I

Better

I've fought wars
To stay alive
A new day
A new fight

Every night the same battle
Pushing aside the darkness
Stand up, not give up

Easier to let go
Easier to let the voices win
Easier to sit and cry
Easier to let go of me

I want to be better
I must be better
I will keep doing better
Alive for one more day

Run, hide

I am running through a forest at night
It's dark and it's raining
I can hear lightning too
I keep running through the dark

I fall, it hurts
I must have cut myself
I see no injury
I get up, keep running

Noises are chasing me
I hear them but I can't see them
Run, run, find a place to hide, be safe
Don't look back, run

End of a mountain
I hear the noise of water, a lake
I hear the voices coming
Jump, they say, jump

The noises approach
The fear makes me jump
I scream but no sound comes out
I hit something hard
I open my eyes,
A nightmare

I'm in my bed, lights off
In my bed, safe
Wait
I hear noises outside
The dark is still there
No place to run, to hide
To be safe

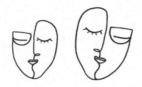

SOBRE MI ANSIEDAD, LA CUARENTENA,
Y ESTE LIBRO

ABOUT BEING IN QUARANTINE, MY
ANXIETY, & THIS BOOK

13 de mayo del 2020 a las 7:44 p.m. Estoy
sentada en la cama con la computadora en
mi falda. La televisión está prendida y mi
celular está al lado mío. Mi madre está en
la sala viendo televisión. Yo lucho con mis
pensamientos tratando de decidir qué escribir.
Es difícil.

El domingo 22 de marzo del 2020 a las 8:00
p.m. empezó la "PAUSA" en Nueva York. Sólo
los trabajadores esenciales podrían salir
a trabajar. Como artista independiente que
trabaja en teatro, cine y televisión esto
significaba que estaría sin trabajo por un
tiempo, lo que ahora parece ser una eternidad,
pues al escribir esto sigo sin trabajo y ya
estamos en mayo.

Durante todo este tiempo he visto artistas y
colegas maravillosos siendo productivos en
medio de la cuarentena. Haciendo "live videos"
en las redes sociales, creando contenido,
haciendo música, horneando, cocinando...
mientras que yo estoy completamente bloqueada.
Siento que me perdí. ¿Cómo puedo llamarme
artista si ni siquiera puedo crear algo?

Cuando todo esto comenzó todos mis demonios
y mis miedos salieron, estaban vivos de
nuevo. Sus voces se volvieron más fuertes y
me paralizaron. Estaba en la casa estancada
siendo poco o nada creativa. Estaba preocupada
y con mucho miedo. No me sentía como yo. Así
pasé las primeras dos a tres semanas hasta
que me di cuenta de que muchas personas,
llenándose de gran valor, comenzaron a
compartir sus problemas de ansiedad y ataques
de pánico en las redes sociales.

Ahí me di cuenta de que todo este tiempo
llevaba ahogada en mi ansiedad y en mis miedos
preocupada por qué hacer y qué historia contar
en vez de simplemente crear, soltarlo todo
y escribir. Poner todo lo que está dentro
de mí en un papel. Así fue como nació este
libro. En medio de profundas ansiedades y

miedos y durante una pandemia, pero desde una
gran necesidad de expresarme y liberar mis
pensamientos.

* * * * * * * *

May 13th, 2020 at 7:44pm. I sit on the bed
with my laptop on my lap. I have my cell phone
next to me. My Mom is in the living room
watching TV. I'm struggling with my thoughts
trying to decide what to write.

On Sunday, March 22nd, 2020 at 8pm New York
entered a "Pause.". Only essential workers
could go to work. As an artist and freelancer
who works in theater, film, and television,
this meant I was going to be out of a job for
a while. This now seems like forever, it's
already May, and this is still happening. I
was struggling a lot when all this started to
happen. I was seeing all these amazing artists
and friends being productive at home, posting
content on social media, creating videos,
music, and baking, while I was completely
blocked and feeling so lost.

How can I consider myself to be an artist if
I can't even create? When this started, all
my demons and my fears came to life and their
voices got stronger. I was paralyzed, stuck.
I felt uncreative, worried, and afraid. I was
not feeling like myself. These feelings lasted
for the first 2 to 3 weeks. Then I started
to see other people being brave enough to
post about their anxiety and panic attacks on
social media and it finally hit me.

All this time I was drowning in anxiety and
fear thinking about what to create instead
of just doing it. Instead of just writing
and letting go, not worrying so much about
what stories to tell but just putting down
everything I was thinking on a blank page.
This is how this book was born. It was born
out of anxiety, in the middle of my fears,
during a pandemic but following a huge need to
express myself through my thoughts.

He intentado varias veces y con varias personas lograr terminar este libro y no he podido. Me siento y no escribo nada. Siento que me he fallado. Una de las cosas que me pasa cuando no logro escribir, o cuando la comunicación con alguien no fluye, es que pienso que es por mi culpa. Por algo que hice o dije. Siempre me culpo y esto ha provocado que se detenga mi proceso creativo. Esto hace que me den ganas de tirar la toalla y que piense que mi visión, mi arte, no tiene propósito, no tiene sentido.

¿Por qué te cuento esto? Tengo dos razones. Una es para que todas aquellas personas que no sufren de ansiedades puedan entender el mundo y la mente de una persona con ansiedad, y con trastorno de ansiedad social -como yo-. La otra razón y la más importante, es porque quiero ayudar a todas aquellas personas que sí sufren de ansiedad dejándoles saber que no están solos.

El ejercicio de escribir este libro me ha ayudado a entender la importancia de detenerse, estar en el momento, analizar lo que pasa por la mente, pensar en lo que sucede dentro de uno para así poder seguir. Esto se debe aplicar a todo lo que hacemos. Hoy más que nunca en estos tiempos de pandemia hay que tratar de vivir un día a la vez porque la incertidumbre se vuelve nuestro día a día. La incertidumbre provoca ansiedad y hay que de alguna manera conseguir fuerzas para seguir y tener paciencia y algún tipo de fé de que vendrán tiempos mejores. Yo no me rendiré, y te invito a que tú no te rindas tampoco. ¡Seguimos!

I have sat down so many times to finish
this book. I have tried so many times and
I've reached out to so many people to help
me finish it and nothing happens. When I
don't get a reply from people and there's
miscommunication, I blame myself. I think
I did or said something that caused this to
happen and I feel that I've failed myself.
Because of my anxiety disorder I tend to
hold myself creatively. I lose interest and
desire. I want to "retire" from anything
creative, because I feel my vision, my art,
has no purpose, no sense.

Why am I telling you this? I have two
reasons. The first one is for people without
anxiety disorder to understand the mind of
the person who deals with it and what goes
through their mind. The other reason and the
most important one, is to help people with
Anxiety Disorders know they are not alone.
In general and deep down in my soul I have
the desire to help those people who don't
suffer from Anxiety Disorders understand what
goes through an anxious mind, and for those
who do suffer from it, tell you we are in
this together.

Anxiety blocks you. It makes you think about
your feelings and why you are feeling them.
When this happens, I try my best to go beyond
the current anxiety moment. When this happens
It's important to think, to analyze and to
understand the moment. Now more than ever
-and especially during a pandemic- we need
to live one day at a time. The reality is
we live in uncertainty. Uncertainty is an
ongoing thing. One needs to have patience and
some kind of faith to know everything will
someday somehow get better. I won't give up.
And I ask you to not give up either. Let's
keep going.

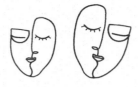

Acknowledgments / Agradecimientos

Yo quiero decir ¡gracias! Gracias por comprar el libro, gracias por leerlo y gracias por tu apoyo. Tengo muchas personas a quienes agradecer. A mis amistades, mi familia, mis mentores, mis profesores, les quiero dar las gracias por creer en mí incluso cuando yo no creía en mí misma.

* * * * * * * *

I want to say, thank you! Thank you for buying the book, thank you for reading and thank you for the support. Thanks to all my friends, my family, my mentors, my former professors, for always believing in me even when I didn't believe in myself.

Special thanks

I want to take a moment to thank those who contribute to the book.

I want to thank my friend Valeria Bosch. Gracias Valeria por leer esas primeras páginas no editas y darme las primeras palabras de aliento y apoyo para continuar escribiendo y para hacer realidad lo que es hoy este libro. ¡Gracias!

I want to thank my friend Rachel Navarro (aka Leaveascar) for her support and contribution to this book and thank you for being part of the song with Moni Meish and I.

I want to thank my friend Quameisha Moreno (aka Moni Meish) for her support and contribution to the book since day 1. You encouraged me to write the first English poems. I was overwhelmed with anxiety and you said write 10 poems today and I wrote all the poems that day. The first part of the book was born in a day full of anxiety. So, thank you. Thank you for the idea and realization of the song. It brought another media and another art to express Anxiety. Thank you.

I want to thank former Professor Helen Huff for saying yes to reading the book and writing her thoughts to be used for the book. I appreciate your time and your feedback. Thank you Professor Huff.

Last, but not least, I want to thank former Professor Arnaldo Bueso for his contribution to the book and especially his contribution on the book title. ¡Gracias!

Mami,

Querida Mami, quiero agradecerte por la vida,
la crianza, las experiencias. Siempre le doy
gracias a la vida porque eres mi Mamá. Estos
últimos 4 años sin papi no han sido fáciles,
pero al estar aquí conmigo, hemos podido
apoyarnos, y seguir adelante, juntas. Tengo
una lista grandísima de agradecimientos,
pero, sobre todo, te agradezco a ti.
Agradezco tu ayuda en mis episodios de
ansiedad. Tú me entiendes, me escuchas y
me das mi espacio. Vivir con alguien con
trastorno múltiple de ansiedad no es fácil,
pero tú no te quitas e intentas entender
lo que pasa por mi cabeza y ayudarme a
controlarlo. Espero que siempre sepas que te
amo y que estaré aquí hasta que Dios diga.

Los terapistas y personas cercanas me han
preguntado si pienso en el suicidio. Los
pensamientos suicidas son a veces parte de
las enfermedades mentales, y aunque a veces
pienso cómo sería no sentir todo esto, cómo
sería callar estas voces y apagar todos
estos sentimientos, mi respuesta siempre es
la misma: no. Nunca lo he considerado. Lo he
pensado, pero nunca lo he considerado porque
jamás podría hacerlo sabiendo el dolor que
sentirías, el dolor que te provocaría, eso sí
que no me lo perdonaría. Tú y mi familia me
sostienen para que no deje que la ansiedad me
controle por completo. Te amo, mami. Gracias.

Dear Mom,

I want to thank you for giving me life, for
the way you raised me, for our experiences
together. I've always thanked the universe
and life because I have you as my mom. These
last 4 years haven't been easy without dad,
but you've been here with me and we are there
for each other continuing to move forward
together. I have a big list of people and
things I am grateful for, but I am especially
thankful for you. For your help during my
anxiety attacks, for your understanding,
for listening to me, for giving me space and
helping me through my episodes. Living with
a person who suffers from anxiety it's not an
easy thing to do, and you do try to help me
as much as you can. I hope you always know
that I love you and I'm here for you.

I've had therapists and close friends ask
me if I've ever considered suicide. I know
suicidal thoughts are something that comes
with mental illness, and even though I
sometimes like to imagine how it would be to
not feel this way anymore, to not hear the
voices and feel all these feelings, my answer
has always been the same one: no. I have not
considered it, not once. I have thought about
it, yes, but I've never considered it to be
an option for me. Why? Because I could never
do it knowing the pain you would feel, the
pain I would cause you, I could never forgive
myself for it. You, mom, you, and my family
are the ones that keep me going and your love
helps me go through my life without letting
anxiety control me completely.
I love you, mom.

A mi familia / To my family

A mi familia en Puerto Rico,

Amo mi infancia en la isla. Amo haber crecido ahí junto a ustedes. Los extraños. Extraño a mi familia. Es lo más difícil de vivir tan lejos, no poder compartir con ustedes tanto como yo quisiera. Los amo.

To my family in New York,

I love you and I am so glad to have you all in my life. I appreciate your support and love. Even though I grew up in Puerto Rico, I remember spending summers in New York and getting to know you. Spending time with you made those summers unforgettable. I love you all.

Papi,

No puedo describir la falta que me haces. El 20 de septiembre del 2020 se cumplieron 4 años sin ti y me parece que fue ayer. Quiero que sepas que estoy bien y que intento seguir luchando tal como me enseñaste. Después de alguien fallecer, siempre me decías: "la vida se acaba para el muerto, el vivo tiene que seguir viviendo." Y eso intento, papi, seguir viviendo. No te niego que te extraño. Extraño tu voz, tus abrazos, tus chistes. Pero seguiré viviendo y quiero que el día que te vuelva a ver, tengamos una conversación larga de contarte todo. Te amo, papi. Te quiero de aquí a la luna.

* * * * * * * *

Dad,

I can't describe how much I miss you. This past September 20th, 2020 will be 4 years without you. It feels like it happened yesterday. I want you to know I am okay and that I keep trying to fight and live just like you taught me. Whenever someone died, you used to say "life is over for the dead, the living has to continue to live." I am trying, dad. I am trying to continue to live. I won't deny how much I miss you. I miss your voice, your hugs, and your jokes. But I will continue to live and when we meet again someday, I want to have a lot to tell you and have a long conversation. I love you, dad. I love you from here to the moon.

How do I begin to thank the person who believed in my work from the moment I shared the idea with her?

This is the first time I share my poems and my thoughts. Many times Anxiety told me to be fearful about sharing. I would expect people's words to say "this is bad, this sucks, you are wasting my time with this", and so I never did.

But this time was different. I took courage to share my work and give myself another chance. Alejandra, you did not only edit grammar and gave logic to my thoughts and words but elevated my work. My book started to take shape. It began to look real and beautiful because of you. You put your work and creativity to it. It has been an honor to work with you. I enjoyed the journey. I learned from it. I've identified my mistakes and now I know what I need to keep growing. I've seen the attention you put into detail and I thank you for it. I am a better writer because of you.

This book it's personal and it is raw. It has been both exciting and scary to let someone into my mind and my world. You were exactly the editor I needed. I thank you and I can't wait to work with you again. ¡Gracias!

Sincerely,
Lucy

About the Editor

ALEJANDRA RAMOS RIERA is a Puerto Rican published playwright, actress and director based in NYC. Winner of The Miranda Family Voces Latinx National Playwriting Competition (2020) with her play Malas mañas. Author of "En la azotea, 10 piezas cortas de teatro" (Ed. Callejón 2016). Playwright-In-Residence at Teatro Publico, Inc., and collaborating artist at Pregones/PRTT.

She holds a B.A in Dance and Theater, from University of Puerto Rico, and a M.A. in Scenic Arts from the University of Murcia, Spain.

Contact:
IG: @aleramosriera
Email: ramos.alejandra1986@gmail.com

Writing is not an easy task. Being an artist is not an easy task. It requires an enormous amount of discipline, consistency, focus and introspection. The action of facing a blank page often feels like jumping from a cliff. I do not suffer from any kind of Anxiety Disorder and I can only imagine what it takes to write a book for those who do suffer from it. The idea alone of engaging in such an enterprise while struggling with mental illness it's not only challenging but incredibly courageous, plausible and admirable.

When Lucy first approached me to see if I was willing and able to edit her book I immediately asked her to send me some excerpts from her manuscript to know if this was something I'd be interested in doing. She ended up sharing the entire book and it took me only five pages to know what my answer was and of course it was yes. I proudly accepted to edit this book because it's daring, unapologetic, raw, and talks not only about her reality but the reality of approximately 40 million American adults who suffer from Anxiety Disorders.

This book is a testimony of what is like to endure mental illness or emotional health problems while diving into a creative process. I find it to be a generous gift that will help a lot of people feel seen, heard, and know they are not alone.

Note to the Illustrator, Amy Cabrero

Amy,
Thank you for the way you brought life into my book. I am grateful and thankful for your work and interpretation of the book through your illustrations.

Amy,
Gracias por tan hermoso trabajo, y la manera que le diste vida a mi libro a través de tus ilustraciones. Y estoy agradecida por tu trabajo y tu arte. ¡Gracias!

Note to the Design Director, Jeniffer Pace

Jeniffer,
Thank you for your work of getting the book into an actual book shape. Thank you for your dedication and enthusiasm.

Jeniffer,
Gracias por tu trabajo. Y por tu paciencia en mis miles de emails y ayudarme en el proceso de darle forma a este libro. Tu dedicación, tu entusiasmo y buena energía me encanto. ¡Gracias!

Lucy Caraballo is a native of Puerto Rico based in New York City who graduated from Lehman College (CUNY) with a BA in Theatre and a minor in Film and Television Studies. She recently worked as an Usher in the "42nd season of the Big Apple Circus" (2019-2020).

She worked as Production Coordinator in the independent feature film "Inside the Circle" (2018) directed by Javier Colon Rios. She worked as Production Assistant in the short film "The Great Alex Fisher" (2018) directed also by Javier Colon Rios, and in the short musical "Talk About It" (2018) directed by Susana Matos Allongo. A Dresser in the production "The Little Mermaid" (2018). And a Stitcher in two national tours: "Gentleman's Guide to Love & Murder" and "The Sound of Music." (2017).

Other related experience includes, Assistant Director and Costume Designer for "Glorious Gloria" at The Gloria Maddox Theatre (2016). Associate costume designer for "Elvira" at Long Island University (2016). Assistant Wardrobe Supervisor for "Measure for Measure" at Tribeca Performing Arts Center (2016). Assistant Director for "The Complete Works of Shakespeare (Abridged)" at BMCC Black Box (2015). Assistant Director for "DNA" at BMCC Black Box (2015) & "Hot L Baltimore" at The Gloria Maddox Theatre (2015). Costume Design Assistant for "The Future Freaks Me Out" at BMCC Black Box (2014) & "The Fairytale Project" at Tribeca Performing Arts Center (2015). Costume Designer for "The Complete Works of Shakespeare (Abridged)" (2015) and "DNA" (2015).

She has also worked as a Background Actor in films and TV shows such as: "New Amsterdam", "Hightown", "Pose", "The Hunt", "Mr. Robot", "Manifest", "Billions", and in Lin-Manuel Miranda's movie "In the Heights."

Lucy volunteered as an usher for the Media Summit of NALIP (National Association of Latino Independent Producers) in Los Angeles, CA (2018). And for Loisaida Center in New York City (2014).

In 2015 she participated in a workshop at the Puerto Rican Traveling Theatre Playwright Unit (Beginners/ Intermediate Unit), which lasted a few months and ended with a stage reading in May 2015.

She is also a Photographer, visit her Instagram page for her photography work.

Lucy has a Podcast named "The 7pm Café Podcast" it is a Podcast about interviewing Artists and it includes episodes on Mental Health.

Lucy has always had a passion for writing, this is her first book.

* * * * * * * * * * * *

Contact:
Instagram: @by.lucycaraballo
E-Mail: by.lucycaraballo@gmail.com

POV: Anxiety

POV: Anxiety is an original song by Moni Meish, Lucy Rivers, Leaveascar, and produced by AOA, in collaboration with this book. In this song, you will hear 3 women creatively recite their point of views (POV) on anxiety.

La canción POV: Anxiety fue inspirada y escrita después de que habláramos del libro y sobre la Ansiedad.

About the artists

Moni Meish:

Quameisha Moreno aka Moni Meish is an Artist from Long Island and The South Bronx. Her musical style is alternative in all genres because her approach comes from her life experiences as an Afro Latinx Female, along with her background in theatre and education, etc.

You can find her music on all platforms by searching Moni Meish. Find her on social Media as Moni Meish as well.

Leaveascar:

Rachel Navarro aka Leaveascar is an artist from the Bronx. She writes and produces music, has acted on screen (T-Mobile Latino/The Sinner), and is a 2X Award-Winning Filmmaker.

Find her on Instagram @leaveascarr
TikTok/YouTube @leaveascar
Listen to her on any music platform as Leaveascar

Lucy Rivers:

Lucy Caraballo aka Lucy Rivers is a Puerto Rican artist from New York. POV: Anxiety is Lucy's first song.

Find her on Instagram: @lucyriversmusic
Spotify: Lucy Rivers

Moni Meish - Verse 1

It's like I'm losing my mind
Like I'm running out of time
Why am I crying all the damn time?
I don't even know what's wrong
All I wanna do is phone
But that attitude I won't condone
You be yellin',
You be screamin',
You be pressin' me
I swear to God
You was born just to stress me
Then I pack it up and say that I'm leavin'
And you say that you need me
And now I'm stuck here.
Damn.

You don't even understand
These different color demons in my head
I gotta get them out,
So I scream and shout...
I want them dead
But you don't hear a thing that I said
It's 1:10am and maybe I…
Just maybe…
I should be dead

Chorus (2x) - Moni Meish, Leaveasca

I can't breathe
I can't breathe
What's it gonna take
For me to be seen?

Leaveascar - Verse 2

Captain of the ship sailing through the seas
I hear greatness calling for me
Letting fear go, remembering to breathe
I escaped death by the skin of my teeth
See the problem is making it about me
There's an 'I' in the middle of anxiety

Don't dim your light 'cause others
don't want to see
most of them try to drive from the backseat
Chorus (2x) - Leaveascar, Lucy Rivers

I can't breathe
I can't breathe
What's it gonna take
For me to be seen?

Lucy Rivers - Bridge

Las voces me hablan
The voices speak
No puedo pararlas
I can't stop them
El miedo me mata
Fear is killing me
El silencio me acompaña
Silence is my companion

Chorus (2x) - Moni Meish, Leaveascar, Lucy Rivers

I can't breathe
I can't breathe
What's it gonna take
For me to be seen?

* * * * * * * * * * * *

You can find the song on any of the following
music platforms:

POV: Anxiety by Moni Meish, Leaveascar, Lucy
Rivers

- Spotify
- Youtube Music
- Amazon Music
- Apple Music